The Wealth Formula

What Black America Can Learn from Jewish Success

First published by Onni's Empire Publishing 2025

Copyright © 2025 by Tiana Brooks

All rights reserved. No part of this publication may be reproduced, stored or transmitted in any form or by any means, electronic, mechanical, photocopying, recording, scanning, or otherwise without written permission from the publisher. It is illegal to copy this book, post it to a website, or distribute it by any other means without permission.

Tiana Brooks asserts the moral right to be identified as the author of this work.

Tiana Brooks has no responsibility for the persistence or accuracy of URLs for external or third-party Internet Websites referred to in this publication and does not guarantee that any content on such Websites is, or will remain, accurate or appropriate.

Designations used by companies to distinguish their products are often claimed as trademarks. All brand names and product names used in this book and on its cover are trade names, service marks, trademarks and registered trademarks of their respective owners. The publishers and the book are not associated with any product or vendor mentioned in this book. None of the companies referenced within the book have endorsed the book.

Legal and Moral Disclaimer

This book is intended for educational and informational purposes only. It is not financial, legal, or investment advice. Readers should conduct their own research and seek professional guidance before making any financial decisions.

The information presented is based on publicly available research, historical data, and cultural analysis. While every effort has been made to ensure accuracy, the author and publisher do not guarantee the completeness or reliability of the information provided.

This book is not an attack on any racial, religious, or ethnic group. It is an analysis of wealth-building strategies and economic patterns, offering insights that may be beneficial for financial empowerment.

The comparisons made in this book are intended to be educational, not divisive. The goal is to encourage learning, adaptation, and strategic action, not to promote stereotypes or resentment.

By reading this book, you agree that the author and publisher are not responsible for any personal, financial, or legal outcomes resulting from the application of the concepts discussed.

First edition

This book was professionally typeset on Reedsy.
Find out more at reedsy.com

Contents

Preface	iv
Introduction: "Wait... So We Could've Been Rich This Whole...	v
Chapter 1: Wealth Is Built, Not Given	1
Chapter 2: The Business Mindset & Ownership Culture	7
Chapter 3: The Power of Community Economics	13
Chapter 4: How Education Is Viewed Differently	20
Chapter 5: Family Structure & Marriage Mindset	27
Chapter 6: Breaking Out of the Paycheck-to-Paycheck Trap	34
Chapter 7: The Role of Faith & Cultural Identity in Success	41
Chapter 8: Moving Forward – Real Strategies for Change	46
Conclusion: They Did It. So Can We.	53

Preface

For generations, Black communities have been told to work hard, get a good job, and hope for the best—while other communities have been strategically building generational wealth behind the scenes.

Jewish families, despite facing discrimination and adversity, have engineered financial security through education, business ownership, strategic spending, and community economics. Meanwhile, Black communities have been trapped in paycheck-to-paycheck survival, student loan debt, and economic instability—not because of a lack of talent or ambition, but because of a lack of strategy, access, and generational knowledge.

This book is not about blaming or begging. It's about understanding what works—and doing something about it.

The information in these pages is meant to be empowering, not discouraging. It is not about comparing who "has it worse" or debating historical injustices—it is about learning from proven wealth-building models and applying them in a way that benefits future generations.

Jewish communities did not wait for fairness—they built their own paths. Black communities must do the same.

This book lays out the blueprint—but reading it isn't enough. It's time to execute.

Introduction: "Wait... So We Could've Been Rich This Whole Time?"

Imagine waking up one morning, checking your bank account, and seeing an extra zero at the end. No fraud alert, no scam—just straight-up generational wealth waiting for you. Sounds like a dream, right? Well, for a lot of Jewish families, it's not a dream—it's a plan. A well-oiled, time-tested, meticulously executed plan.

Meanwhile, in too many Black families, financial discussions sound more like:

- *"Money don't grow on trees."*
- *"God will provide."*
- *"Just work twice as hard and hope for the best."*
- *"Oh, and if you do get some money, make sure you don't let your family find out, or you'll be everybody's personal ATM."*

Somewhere along the way, two communities—both historically oppressed, both facing discrimination, both surviving against ridiculous odds—ended up on two very different financial paths. And no, it's not because Jewish people had it easy (spoiler alert: they didn't). It's because their families were playing chess while too many of us were stuck playing the lottery.

This Ain't a Sob Story—It's a Playbook

This book isn't here to complain. It's not a "woe is me" pity party about why Black folks have struggled financially in America. Instead, think of this as the economic masterclass you never got in school—except it's funny, painfully real, and will probably make you say, *"Damn, we really been doing it all wrong."*

See, Jewish families didn't stumble into wealth by accident. They didn't wake up one day and say, "You know what? Let's just start owning banks, running Hollywood, and dominating real estate." Nah, this was intentional generational planning— something Black communities have struggled with for a long list of historical, systemic, and cultural reasons.

- Jewish families teach financial literacy from day one. Black families? We get taught how to survive, but rarely how to build wealth.
- Jewish families pass down businesses and assets. Black families? Some of us are just hoping Big Mama doesn't lose the house to unpaid property taxes.
- Jewish communities circulate money within their own people. Black communities? Our money leaves so fast it's like it saw a ghost.

It's time we stop fighting against facts and start learning from what works—without making excuses, without blaming anyone, and without feeling like sellouts for saying, *"Hey, maybe we should copy the people who figured this money thing out."*

If They Can Do It, So Can We

This book is going to break down exactly how Jewish families build, protect, and pass down wealth—and how Black communities can start doing the same. We're going to laugh, we're going to cringe at some hard truths, and by the end, we're going to have a blueprint that actually works.

Because let's be real—nobody wants to be broke. But without a strategy, wealth is just a dream. And if there's one thing we've learned from Jewish families, it's that wealth isn't dreamed—it's planned.

Chapter 1: Wealth Is Built, Not Given

(*Or: Why Praying for a Financial Miracle Ain't a Retirement Plan*)

If you grew up in a Black household, chances are you heard some version of this speech when money got tight:

- *"God will make a way."*
- *"Just be grateful for what you got."*
- *"Money comes and goes."*
- *"These bills gonna be the death of me."*

Meanwhile, Jewish families hear:

- *"Start saving early."*
- *"Never let money sit—make it work for you."*
- *"Own, don't rent."*
- *"Invest in your people first."*

See the difference? Both groups believe in faith, resilience, and hard work, but one community strategizes money like chess, while the other has historically been denied access to the game board altogether.

Let's break it down:

1. The Wealth Gap: How Two Oppressed Groups Took Two Different Paths

Jewish people and Black Americans both faced severe discrimination in the U.S. But the economic results look vastly different today:

- Median Jewish household wealth (2019): $440,000+
- Median Black household wealth (2019): $24,100
- Percentage of Jewish households earning $100K+ per year: 44%
- Percentage of Black households earning $100K+ per year: 14%

(Source: Federal Reserve, Pew Research Center)

These numbers didn't happen by accident. One community focused on long-term financial security—despite facing anti-Semitic restrictions, expulsions, and targeted violence. The other was systematically blocked from wealth-building for centuries.

- Redlining & Housing Discrimination: Black Americans were locked out of real estate ownership (the #1 driver of middle-class wealth) while Jewish families, though initially discriminated against, were able to secure property in certain neighborhoods and pass it down.
- The GI Bill: After WWII, white and Jewish veterans got home loans and college funding. Black veterans were denied access to these same programs.
- Banking & Lending Discrimination: Jewish families formed their own credit unions and loan networks, while

Black business owners were systematically denied funding.

The result? Jewish wealth circulates within their communities across generations. Meanwhile, Black families are often forced to start from zero, every generation.

2. Wealth Circulation: The 6-Hour Money Problem

This one is a gut-punch.

- The average Jewish dollar circulates 17 to 30 times within the community before leaving.
- The average Black dollar? It's gone in SIX HOURS.

(Source: Nielsen Report, 2019)

Let that sink in. Jewish money bounces around within Jewish-owned banks, businesses, and investments, growing in value before ever reaching outside hands. Black dollars? They take a one-way trip to other communities, making everyone else rich first.

- Example: A Jewish family eats at a Jewish-owned restaurant.
- The restaurant banks with a Jewish-owned financial institution.
- That bank funds a Jewish business owner's new company.
- That company hires Jewish employees, who repeat the cycle.

Now, compare that to a typical Black consumer experience:

- Earn a paycheck → Buy gas at a non-Black-owned station

→ Eat at a non-Black-owned restaurant → Shop at a non-Black-owned store → Pay rent to a non-Black landlord → And... the money is gone.

This isn't a "we need to boycott white businesses" rant. It's a wake-up call. If money doesn't stay and circulate within Black communities, how are we ever supposed to build lasting wealth?

3. Generational Wealth: The Difference Between "Starting Over" and "Starting Ahead"

Ask a 21-year-old Jewish college student what their financial plan is, and they might say:

- "I'm interning at my uncle's firm to gain experience before starting my own business."
- "My parents are helping me buy a condo instead of renting."
- "I have a trust fund to help with grad school."

Now, ask a 21-year-old Black college student, and you might hear:

- "I'm trying to avoid $100K in student debt."
- "I gotta help my family out financially while I'm in school."
- "Once I graduate, I'll just figure it out."

One is planning for the future. The other is already behind before even starting.

- Percentage of Jewish families that leave inheritances: 70%
- Percentage of Black families that leave inheritances: 23%

(*Source: Federal Reserve, 2019*)

Jewish parents aren't just giving handouts—they're strategically setting up their kids with:

- Interest-free loans for first homes.
- Business startup capital.
- Family-run investments.

Meanwhile, too many Black families pass down debt and funeral costs.

And no, this isn't because Jewish people are naturally "better with money." They were shut out of traditional banking systems for centuries, so they built their own. Black Americans? We weren't given that chance—and when we tried (i.e., Black Wall Street), it was literally burned to the ground.

4. Breaking the Cycle: How We Fix This

Here's the part where we stop laughing and start strategizing.

Solution 1: Teach Financial Literacy Early

- Jewish families talk about stocks, credit, and investing at the dinner table.
- Black families? We gotta start doing the same—because schools sure as hell won't.

Solution 2: Stop Flexing, Start Owning

- We can't keep buying liabilities (luxury brands, cars, consumer debt) while ignoring assets (real estate, businesses, investments).
- It's time to invest in what appreciates—not what depreciates the second we leave the store.

Solution 3: Build Our Own Financial Networks

- Jewish communities lend to each other without predatory interest.
- Black communities need to create our own investment circles, group real estate purchases, and community banks.

Solution 4: Create Generational Wealth on Purpose

- We can't keep pushing kids out at 18 with zero financial support and expecting them to "figure it out."
- Even if we're starting from nothing, we can start small—life insurance, investments, and small assets build up over time.

Final Thought: If It's Possible for Them, It's Possible for Us

Nobody's saying Black folks should "act Jewish." This isn't about cultural imitation—it's about economic strategies that work.

- We don't need handouts—we need a blueprint.
- We don't need permission—we need execution.
- We don't need to wish for wealth—we need to build it.

Chapter 2: The Business Mindset & Ownership Culture

(Or: Why Your Job Ain't Gonna Make You Rich, But Ownership Might)

Let's start with a simple but brutal fact:

> *Over 80% of millionaires in America are business owners.*
> *Less than 15% of Black Americans own a business.*

(Source: U.S. Census Bureau, Federal Reserve, 2023)

See the problem? Jewish families teach ownership from childhood. Black families? We've been conditioned to "get a good job" and "play it safe." The problem is, no one gets rich off a paycheck alone.

And before somebody shouts *"But I know Black millionaires with jobs!"*—yes, they exist. But guess what? Most of them own stocks, invest in real estate, or have a business on the side.

So let's talk about how Jewish families ingrain ownership early, why Black families are stuck in the employee mindset, and—most importantly—how we can break the cycle.

1. Jewish Families Teach Ownership, Not Just Employment

Ever heard this classic Black parent speech?

- *"Get a good education so you can get a good job."*
- *"Work twice as hard as white folks to keep your position."*
- *"Don't take risks; make sure you got security."*

Sounds responsible, right? But here's what Jewish families tell their kids:

- *"Learn a high-income skill so you can build your own business."*
- *"If you do work a job, use it to gain experience and then go independent."*
- *"Leverage your network—your connections will help fund your future."*

See the difference? One mindset builds employees. The other builds owners.

Example: Why Jewish People Own, While Black People Rent (Literally & Figuratively)

Jewish Communities:

- The parents own a deli, law firm, or real estate properties.
- They hire their kids to learn business skills young.
- By the time the kid is 25, they either inherit the business or start their own.

CHAPTER 2: THE BUSINESS MINDSET & OWNERSHIP CULTURE

Black Communities:

- The parents tell the kid to get a degree and "work for a good company."
- The kid gets a job, but has no assets or business skills.
- By 25, they're paying rent, drowning in debt, and relying on a paycheck.

Now, before anyone gets mad: this isn't about blaming Black families. It's about understanding the historical setup that put us at a disadvantage.

2. The System Was Rigged—But Now It's Time to Play Smarter

Let's keep it 100: Black entrepreneurship was deliberately sabotaged.

- Black Wall Street (1921): A thriving, wealthy Black business district in Tulsa was literally burned down by racist mobs.
- Racial Zoning Laws (1930s-1960s): Black business owners were blocked from prime real estate while Jewish and other immigrant communities could buy in.
- Banking Discrimination (1950s-2000s): Black business owners were denied loans at higher rates, while Jewish business owners created community-backed funding networks.

(Source: Federal Reserve, Brookings Institute, 2022)

So, while Jewish families were building generational business empires, Black business owners were being shut down, denied loans, or outright destroyed.

But here's the good news: It's 2025. The internet exists. We have more opportunities than ever. The only thing stopping us now is strategy.

3. How Jewish Communities Fund Their Own—And Why Black Entrepreneurs Struggle

Here's another wealth hack Jewish families use: community-backed business funding.

- Need a business loan? Jewish organizations provide low-interest loans to their own people.
- Need investors? They pool money from family and friends.
- Need mentorship? There's an entire network of experienced Jewish entrepreneurs who guide the next generation.

Now, let's talk about Black entrepreneurs.

- Need a business loan? Rejected by the bank.
- Need investors? Nobody in the family has extra money to invest.
- Need mentorship? You're figuring it out alone.

This isn't an excuse—it's a blueprint we can start adopting today.

Action Steps Black Communities Can Take:

- Start Group Economics – Small groups (family, friends, church) can pool money for business loans, real estate, and investments.

- Community Banks & Credit Unions – Move money into Black-owned financial institutions to reinvest in Black businesses.
- Business Incubators – Create local support networks where experienced entrepreneurs guide new ones.

The solution isn't waiting for the system to change. It's building our own system.

4. Why Every Black Family Needs A Business—Even If It's Small

Even if you love your job, having a business gives you options.

- If you get laid off, you still have income.
- If you hate your boss, you can walk away.
- If you need wealth for your kids, you can pass it down.

The 3 Levels of Business Ownership:

1. Side Hustle Level: A small income stream (Airbnb, consulting, online store).
2. Wealth Builder Level: A profitable business that replaces your 9-to-5 job.
3. Legacy Level: A business you pass down to your kids (real estate, law firm, restaurant).

Not everyone has to build a million-dollar empire. But EVERY Black family should own something.

- Even a vending machine is better than nothing.

- Even a rental property is better than nothing.
- Even an Etsy shop is better than nothing.

Start small. But start.

Final Thought: Own SOMETHING, or Be Owned by the System

Black people are some of the most talented, creative, and hard-working people on the planet. The problem isn't ability—it's ownership.

- Jewish families teach "Ownership First."
- Black families teach "Job Security First."

It's time to shift.
If they can do it, so can we.

Chapter 3: The Power of Community Economics

Why Your Dollar Leaves the Hood Before You Even Finish Your Sandwich

Let's start with a hard truth:

If Black Americans were a country, we'd be the 8th richest nation in the world.

Yet, Black communities remain some of the poorest.

(Source: Nielsen Report, 2022)

How is that possible? Because money doesn't stay where it's made.

Jewish money circulates 17-30 times before leaving the community.

Black money? Gone in six hours.

(Source: Brookings Institute, 2023)

Let me put this in perspective:

- You wake up, hit the gas station (non-Black-owned).
- You grab coffee from Starbucks (non-Black-owned).
- You order lunch on Uber Eats (non-Black-owned restaurant, non-Black-owned delivery platform).

- You get paid and send your money straight to Verizon, Amazon, and Netflix (non-Black-owned companies).

Before the day even ends, your dollar has left the community and gone to build someone else's generational wealth.

Meanwhile, Jewish families engineer their spending habits so their money stays in their circle as long as possible.

Let's break this down.

1. How Jewish Communities Keep Their Money "In-House"

The Jewish Business Cycle

Jewish communities operate on a simple but powerful system:

- Jewish people buy from Jewish-owned businesses.
- Jewish businesses bank with Jewish-owned financial institutions.
- Jewish investors fund Jewish entrepreneurs.
- Jewish landlords rent to Jewish tenants.
- Jewish professionals (lawyers, doctors, accountants) serve their own first.

The result? Money stays and grows within the community before it ever leaves.

The Black Spending Cycle (Or Lack Thereof)

Now, let's compare this to a typical Black spending pattern:

- Black people buy from non-Black businesses.
- Black businesses bank with non-Black banks.
- Black investors (the few that exist) rarely fund Black startups.
- Black tenants rent from non-Black landlords.
- Black professionals often have to work outside their community to make money.

See the problem?
 Jewish money builds Jewish wealth.
 Black money builds everyone else's wealth.
 And before someone says, "Well, Black businesses just need to be better," that's not the issue. The issue is habit, trust, and access.

2. Black Wall Street: What We Had (And What Was Taken)

Here's the painful part: Black people did have strong community economics. We just weren't allowed to keep it.

- Greenwood, Tulsa (1921) – The original "Black Wall Street," a thriving district of Black-owned banks, hospitals, and businesses. Burned down in one of the worst race massacres in history.
- Rosewood, Florida (1923) – A self-sustaining Black town destroyed after a false accusation led to white mobs mas-

sacring residents and burning the town.
- Urban Renewal (1950s-1970s) – Black business districts in cities like Chicago, New York, and Atlanta were bulldozed in the name of "development."

(Source: Smithsonian National Museum of African American History, 2022)

While Jewish communities were discriminated against, they were allowed to rebuild. Black communities were wiped out repeatedly.

That's why our economic foundation is weak—we were forcibly prevented from building one.

3. Rebuilding What Was Lost: How Black Communities Can Keep Money Circulating

Jewish communities didn't just "get lucky" with money. They built financial safety nets.

Here's how we can do the same.

1. Move Your Money to Black-Owned Banks

Jewish people don't put their money in banks that don't serve their interests.

If Black Americans shifted just 10% of their deposits to Black-owned banks, we'd increase Black lending power by billions.

Action Step: Find a Black-owned bank near you or open an account at a digital Black-owned bank.

2. Prioritize Black-Owned Businesses

Jewish people intentionally buy from their own businesses first.

Black people need to develop the same mindset—not just for culture, but for economic survival.

Action Step: Next time you shop for something, ask: "Is there a Black-owned business that sells this?"

3. Create Investment Circles

Jewish communities don't rely on outside investors—they fund their own.

They form small investment groups where members pool money for:

- Business startups
- Real estate purchases
- Community development

Action Step: Start a five-to-ten person investment group where each member contributes fifty to one hundred dollars per month toward a shared investment goal.

4. Stop Renting, Start Owning

Jewish families teach real estate ownership from a young age.

- Eighty percent of Jewish households own property.
- Less than forty-five percent of Black households do.

(Source: U.S. Census Bureau, 2023)

Action Step: Even if you can't buy a house yet, start with land, an investment property, or a small stake in a real estate group.

4. Group Economics vs. Individual Success: Why Black Celebrities Ain't Enough

Every time we see a successful Black billionaire, people think we're "winning."

- Jay-Z is a billionaire.
- Oprah is a billionaire.
- LeBron is a billionaire.

Cool. Now name five thriving Black-owned banks.
 Or five major Black-owned grocery chains.
 Or five Black tech companies dominating their industry.
 Exactly.
 Jewish wealth is community wealth.
 Black wealth is individual wealth.
 Jay-Z being rich doesn't change the fact that Black household wealth is shrinking.
 Until we stop celebrating individual success and start focusing on group economics, we'll keep losing the game.

Final Thought: We Don't Need Permission to Build Wealth

Jewish communities made their own rules.
Black communities have waited for the system to be fair.
The system isn't ever going to be fair.
So what's the move? Build our own.

- Buy from your own.
- Bank with your own.
- Invest in your own.
- Own something.

It's not about race—it's about strategy.

Chapter 4: How Education Is Viewed Differently

(*Or: Why Jewish Kids Are Learning About Compound Interest While Black Kids Are Getting Roasted for "Acting White"*)

Education is one of the biggest wealth indicators in America. It's not about just getting a degree—it's about how education is used strategically to build financial security.

Now, let's look at the numbers:

- Jewish Americans have the highest percentage of college graduates among all ethnic groups in the U.S.
- Black Americans have the lowest college completion rate of any racial group.
- Jewish families prioritize specialized, high-earning fields like medicine, law, finance, and business ownership.
- Black students are overrepresented in fields with low financial return and high student debt, like sociology and education.

(Source: U.S. Department of Education, Pew Research Center)

Jewish communities see education as a financial weapon—Black communities have been taught to see it as a generic "way out." One approach builds wealth and stability, the other leads to debt with no clear economic benefit.

Let's break down how Jewish families use education differently and how Black communities can adopt the same strategies.

1. The Jewish Approach: Education Is a Business Strategy

In Jewish culture, education is not just about knowledge—it's about power and financial security.

- Jewish kids are taught early that education is an investment. The goal isn't just to get a diploma—it's to enter high-income, high-security professions.
- They avoid unnecessary student debt. Parents actively guide their kids toward degrees that will pay for themselves within a few years.
- They use family networks to secure jobs. It's not just about getting a degree—it's about using connections to land lucrative careers straight out of school.

Black communities, on the other hand, have been conditioned to believe in education as a "golden ticket" without strategy. The result?

- Black students take on excessive debt for degrees that don't guarantee financial security.
- There's no strategic career planning—many students choose majors without understanding their earning potential.
- No built-in job pipeline—students graduate and have to fight for entry-level jobs with no inside connections.

The difference is intentional strategy versus blind faith in the system.

2. The Trap of Useless Degrees & Student Loan Debt

Let's talk about one of the biggest scams in modern history—the student loan crisis.

- Jewish families avoid student debt at all costs.
- Black families are buried in student debt and told, *"Education is the key to success."*

The result?

- The average Jewish graduate owes significantly less student debt than the national average.
- The average Black graduate owes $52,000 in student loans by age 30 and is struggling to buy a house or build wealth.

(Source: Federal Reserve, National Center for Education Statistics)

Not all degrees are equal. Jewish families steer their kids away from debt-heavy degrees with no return. Black students, on the other hand, are told, *"Follow your passion and the money will come."* That advice has left entire generations broke.

Fields that pay off:

- Law
- Medicine
- Engineering
- Finance

- Real Estate Development
- Business Ownership

Fields that usually don't:

- Psychology
- Sociology
- Communications
- Education
- Fine Arts

This isn't about saying people shouldn't follow their passions—but passion without financial strategy leads to struggle. Jewish parents make sure their kids understand this early.

3. The Pipeline to High-Paying Careers vs. The "Figure It Out" Model

Jewish students don't just graduate and hope for the best—they are plugged into a structured career pipeline before they even finish school.

- Jewish students are mentored by professionals in their community before they even choose a major.
- Internships and job placements are secured through family and community networks.
- If they can't find a job, they are funded to start their own businesses.

Meanwhile, in Black communities:

- Mentorship is rare. Most students are first-generation graduates with no guidance on how to leverage their degree.
- Job connections are limited. There is no built-in job pipeline—graduates are left to fight for positions with no competitive advantage.
- Entrepreneurship isn't an option. Jewish students graduate with financial backing to start a business if they can't find a job—Black students graduate with debt.

This is why so many Black graduates end up underemployed despite having degrees. It's not just about going to school—it's about learning how to turn that education into generational wealth.

4. The Education Fix: How Black Families Can Use School as a Wealth Tool

1. Stop Taking on Debt for Degrees That Don't Pay

- If a degree doesn't have high earning potential, it's not worth six figures in loans.
- Community college for general education credits is a smart move before transferring to a bigger university.
- Trade schools and certifications often lead to high-paying jobs with less debt than a traditional degree.

2. Push Kids Toward Strategic Careers, Not Just College for the Sake of College

- Encourage careers that lead to business ownership or high salaries.
- Help students understand what degrees actually pay off before they commit to student loans.

3. Create a Career Pipeline for the Next Generation

- Jewish communities set their kids up for job placement—Black communities can do the same by building professional mentorship networks.
- Every successful Black professional should commit to mentoring at least one young person to ensure career continuity.

4. Teach Financial Literacy Alongside Academics

- Jewish kids learn about investing, saving, and credit early.
- Black students need the same education before they even get their first paycheck.

Final Thought: Education Without Strategy Is Just Debt

Jewish communities use education as a tool for wealth-building—Black communities have been tricked into using it as a tool for survival.

It's time to change the game.

- Don't take on debt without a plan.

- Don't chase a degree just for the sake of it.
- Use education as a financial weapon—not just a piece of paper.

We don't need more Black students in college. We need more Black students in fields that build generational wealth.

And if Jewish families can engineer their kids' success with strategic education, Black families can do the same.

Chapter 5: Family Structure & Marriage Mindset

(Or: Why Jewish Kids Get Down Payments and Black Kids Get "You Grown, Figure It Out")

If you've ever wondered why Jewish families build generational wealth at higher rates than Black families, look no further than family structure and financial planning for marriage.

- Jewish parents invest in their children's future stability.
- Black parents often expect their kids to "make it on their own."
- Jewish families see marriage as an economic foundation.
- Black families have been systematically fractured by policies that discouraged two-parent households.

And before anyone says, *"Marriage doesn't matter,"* let's check the receipts.

- Median net worth of married Black families: $53,000
- Median net worth of single Black households: $7,000

(Source: Federal Reserve, 2022)

That's a sevenfold difference in wealth.

Jewish families engineer their children's financial future by prioritizing marriage, stability, and family wealth planning. Black families, through no fault of their own, have been conditioned to survive independently instead of building generational wealth as a unit.

Let's break down how Jewish families create financial security through marriage and family structure—and what Black communities can do to rebuild what was lost.

1. Jewish Families Treat Marriage Like a Business—Because It Is

In Jewish culture, marriage isn't just about love—it's about economic partnership.

- Marriages are arranged with long-term financial goals in mind.
- Families provide financial support to help young couples buy homes.
- Children are expected to marry within the faith to maintain economic stability.

Contrast this with modern Black marriage culture, which has been deeply affected by systemic destruction of the Black family.

- Slavery split Black families apart.
- Welfare policies in the 1960s punished two-parent Black households.
- Mass incarceration removed Black men from families, forcing single motherhood to become the norm.

(Source: U.S. Census Bureau, 2023)

Jewish families have preserved marriage as an economic strategy. Meanwhile, Black families have been forced into a culture of financial independence out of necessity.

2. The Financial Benefits of Marriage That Jewish Families Leverage

Jewish communities understand that marriage is a financial advantage. Here's why:

1. Two Incomes Build Wealth Faster Than One

- A married couple saves money on housing, utilities, and expenses.
- Single people pay 60% more per person on average for the same lifestyle.

(Source: Pew Research, 2022)

2. Children in Two-Parent Homes Have Higher Economic Stability

- Jewish parents pass down wealth, assets, and businesses to their children.
- Black children are more likely to grow up in single-parent households, leading to lower economic stability.

The difference is planning. Jewish families set up financial safety nets to ensure their kids never start from zero.

3. The Down Payment Secret: How Jewish Parents Set Up Their Kids for Success

One of the biggest financial advantages Jewish families give their children? They help them buy homes early.

- Jewish parents often gift or loan their children money for a down payment.
- Homeownership is one of the fastest paths to wealth, and Jewish families make sure their kids get a head start.

Now, let's compare:

- 70% of Jewish families own homes.
- Less than 45% of Black families own homes.

(Source: U.S. Census Bureau, 2023)

This isn't because Jewish people "got lucky." It's because their families invested in long-term stability.

Meanwhile, in Black communities:

- Many young adults are forced to rent indefinitely.
- Parents expect their children to be financially independent from day one.
- The "18 and you're grown" mentality leaves Black kids starting from scratch.

The result? Black wealth is constantly being reset instead of being passed down.

4. Breaking the Cycle: How Black Families Can Rebuild Financially Stable Households

1. Change the Narrative Around Marriage

Jewish families expect their kids to marry early and smart. Black families have been conditioned to think:

- *"Marriage is optional."*
- *"Love should come before finances."*
- *"It's better to be independent."*

But independence is expensive. Building wealth as a team is far more powerful than struggling alone.

2. Support Young Couples Financially (Where Possible)

- If Jewish families can help their children buy homes, Black families can start small by helping with credit, investments, or savings.
- Even $5,000 toward a down payment can make the difference between renting for life or owning a home.

3. Rebuild Black Business and Inheritance Culture

- Jewish families leave their children businesses, investments, and real estate.
- Black families must start planning inheritances, even if it's small.

If you can't leave money, leave knowledge.

If you can't leave a house, leave investment skills.

5. Family Wealth Planning: The Jewish Blueprint That Works

Jewish families actively plan wealth for the next generation. Here's how:

- They create family trusts.
- They invest in insurance policies.
- They ensure assets are passed down properly.

Black families, by contrast, often don't plan for wealth transfer at all.

- Many Black families don't have wills.
- Many Black-owned homes are lost due to unpaid taxes.
- Generational wealth disappears instead of being maintained.

This can change today.

Action Steps for Black Families to Start Now

- Set up a will and life insurance policy. Protect assets before it's too late.
- Start family investment accounts. Even small contributions grow over time.
- Educate children on wealth management. Break the cycle of financial illiteracy.

Final Thought: Marriage and Family Are Economic Weapons—Use Them

Jewish families engineer their children's success. Black families have been forced into economic survival mode. It's time to change that.

- Marriage builds wealth faster than singlehood.
- Parental financial planning sets the next generation up for success.
- Strategic family wealth transfer is how legacies are built.

Black communities don't need more struggle stories. We need financially equipped families.

Chapter 6: Breaking Out of the Paycheck-to-Paycheck Trap

(*Or: Why Jewish Families Build Generational Wealth While Black Families Are One Emergency Away from Broke*)

If you've ever felt like you work too damn hard to be this broke, you're not alone.

- 60% of Black Americans live paycheck to paycheck.
- Only 9% of Jewish households report living check to check.
- The median Black household has less than $1,500 in savings.
- The median Jewish household has over $50,000 in liquid assets.

(Source: Federal Reserve, Pew Research Center)

Jewish families aren't just better at making money—they're better at keeping it.

Meanwhile, Black communities have been conditioned to spend every dollar they earn, leading to a cycle of financial stress, debt, and dependence on unstable jobs.

This chapter is about how Jewish families escape the paycheck trap—and how Black communities can do the same.

CHAPTER 6: BREAKING OUT OF THE PAYCHECK-TO-PAYCHECK TRAP

1. Jewish Families View Money as a Tool—Black Families Have Been Taught to See It as Temporary

Ever heard these phrases growing up?

- *"You can't take it with you when you die."*
- *"Live for today, worry about tomorrow later."*
- *"As long as the bills are paid, I'm good."*

Now, compare that to the Jewish financial mindset:

- *"Every dollar should be working for you."*
- *"You don't get rich by earning, you get rich by investing."*
- *"You save first, then spend what's left."*

Jewish families treat money like a tool—Black families, largely due to historical oppression, have been conditioned to treat money as something that disappears quickly.

It's not our fault. After centuries of being denied wealth-building opportunities, Black people never got the chance to learn how to make money work long-term.

But we can change that.

2. The Difference Between Jewish and Black Spending Habits

Jewish families and Black families earn money the same way—but they don't use it the same way.

Where the Average Jewish Dollar Goes:

- 20% Investments (stocks, real estate, business ownership)
- 15% Savings (rainy day fund, family trusts)
- 10% Community & Philanthropy
- 10% Business Networking & Development
- 45% Lifestyle Expenses

Where the Average Black Dollar Goes:

- 50% Bills & Debt Payments
- 25% Rent (Instead of Owning)
- 15% Consumer Spending (Brands, Fashion, Entertainment)
- 10% Savings & Investments

(Source: Nielsen Consumer Report, 2023)

Jewish money works for them first before it touches lifestyle expenses.

Black money? It's gone before it has a chance to grow.

This is why a Jewish person can have an average job but still build wealth, while a Black person with the same job is struggling just to survive.

3. How Black Communities Got Trapped in Paycheck-to-Paycheck Living

If you grew up in survival mode, this isn't your fault. The system was built to keep Black people broke.

- Redlining blocked Black families from homeownership.
- Predatory lending trapped Black people in debt cycles.
- Welfare policies penalized Black two-parent households.
- Job discrimination forced many Black workers into lower-paying fields.

(Source: Brookings Institute, U.S. Treasury)

Meanwhile, Jewish families, while also facing discrimination, created their own financial institutions, businesses, and community support systems—ensuring their money stayed in-house.

The good news? You don't need to be born rich to break free from the paycheck cycle.

You just need a strategy.

4. The Jewish Blueprint for Escaping Paycheck-to-Paycheck Living

Jewish families follow a simple but powerful money system.

1. The "Pay Yourself First" Rule

- Before spending a dime, 10-20% of every paycheck goes to savings and investments.
- Black families often pay bills first and save whatever is left

(which is usually nothing).

2. Owning, Not Renting

- Jewish families prioritize homeownership early, even if it means starting small.
- Black families rent longer, which prevents wealth accumulation.

3. Investing as a Non-Negotiable

- Jewish families invest in stocks, real estate, and businesses early in life.
- Black families focus on working hard and saving—but saving alone doesn't build wealth.

4. Avoiding Consumer Debt

- Jewish families avoid debt unless it's for wealth-building.
- Black families are often encouraged to use credit for cars, furniture, and luxury purchases.

5. Multiple Streams of Income

- Jewish families don't rely on a single paycheck.
- Black families are often taught to find a "good job" and stick to it.

It's not about how much you make—it's about how you use it.

5. How Black Communities Can Escape the Paycheck Trap

1. Automate Saving and Investing

- Set up auto-deposits into a savings account before paying bills.
- Invest in low-cost index funds ($50 a month grows to six figures over time).

2. Prioritize Ownership Over Consumption

- Stop financing cars—use that money for a down payment on property.
- Find ways to get out of renting—even a small property is better than renting for life.

3. Create Passive Income Streams

- Start a side business (consulting, e-commerce, content creation).
- Own something that makes money while you sleep (stocks, rental properties).

4. Build Group Economics

- Pool money with trusted friends/family to buy property or start businesses.
- Stop spending every dollar outside the community.

5. Get Out of Survival Mode

- Being broke isn't just a money problem—it's a mindset problem.
- Jewish families teach wealth-building from childhood—Black communities need to do the same.

6. The Final Wealth Formula: How to Go from Paycheck to Freedom

Breaking out of the cycle isn't about making more money.
It's about keeping and growing the money you already have.
The Jewish formula is simple:

1. Save first. Before you spend, put money aside.
2. Invest early. Your money should be making more money.
3. Own something. Rent is a wealth trap.
4. Keep debt low. Never finance what doesn't grow in value.
5. Build multiple income streams. Never rely on one paycheck.

Black communities can apply these same principles today.

Chapter 7: The Role of Faith & Cultural Identity in Success

(*Or: Why Jewish Communities Use Faith to Build Wealth While Black Churches Preach About "Waiting on God"*)

Faith is one of the strongest forces in both Jewish and Black communities.

- Nearly 90% of Jewish households actively practice cultural and religious traditions.
- More than 80% of Black Americans identify as Christian, with Black churches playing a central role in the community.

(Source: Pew Research, 2023)

Yet, there's a huge difference in how faith is used as a tool for financial empowerment.

- Jewish families use faith as a guide for economic planning, wealth-building, and financial responsibility.
- Black churches often promote faith as a tool for endurance, patience, and hope—without practical financial strategies.

This isn't an attack on Black faith—this is about how faith can

be used as an asset rather than just a coping mechanism.
Let's break it down.

1. How Jewish Communities Use Faith to Build Economic Power

In Jewish culture, faith is deeply connected to financial responsibility.

- Tzedakah (Charitable Giving): Jewish families are expected to give back strategically, not just blindly donate.
- Shabbat (Wealth & Rest Balance): Financial discipline includes knowing when to work and when to recharge.
- Torah Teachings on Money: Financial wisdom is passed down through religious study and real-world application.

Jewish communities don't just pray for money—they plan for money using faith as a structured guideline.

Compare this to Black church culture, which often teaches:

- *"God will provide."*
- *"Don't worry about money—trust the Lord."*
- *"If you sow a seed, God will bless you."*

These messages sound good, but without financial action, they leave people waiting instead of building.

2. The Prosperity Gospel Trap: When Faith Is Used Against Black Wealth

Let's address the elephant in the room: Prosperity Gospel.

- The idea that if you give to the church, God will bless you financially
- Encouraging emotional giving instead of strategic investing
- Pastors living in mansions while their congregation struggles

While Jewish communities use faith to build businesses, invest, and pass down wealth, many Black churches have taught people to give without financial wisdom.

This is why you see:

- Million-dollar Black megachurches sitting in poor Black neighborhoods.
- Congregants faithfully tithing while struggling to pay their own bills.
- Black pastors flying private jets while their members take the bus.

This isn't about bashing Christianity—it's about exposing how faith is being misused when it comes to money.

3. The Jewish Approach: Faith + Financial Action

Jewish faith emphasizes God + personal responsibility.

- *"God helps those who help themselves."*

- *"Wealth is a responsibility, not just a blessing."*
- *"Tithing is about community impact, not personal miracles."*

This means Jewish families:

- Tithe and give strategically, making sure money is reinvested in their own community.
- Teach their children financial principles alongside religious values.
- Use faith as motivation to build, not just endure.

4. Reframing Black Faith for Economic Empowerment

Black communities don't need less faith—we need faith with action.

1. Stop Waiting, Start Building

- Faith isn't an excuse to ignore financial planning.
- Stop praying for wealth without strategy.

2. Demand Financial Literacy in the Church

- If your pastor isn't teaching financial empowerment, ask why.
- Churches should be teaching investment, credit management, and ownership.

3. Use Tithing Strategically

- Give to build, not just to survive.
- Black churches should create wealth-building programs, not just take offerings.

4. Teach Biblical Financial Wisdom

- The Bible talks about investing, managing money, and avoiding debt.
- If your church only preaches waiting on God, they're ignoring half the message.

5. The Real Message: Faith + Financial Strategy = Power

Jewish communities don't separate faith from economic planning—they use faith as a framework for financial success.

Black communities can do the same by:

- Using faith to build, not just endure.
- Demanding financial education in religious spaces.
- Combining spiritual wealth with real-world financial power.

Faith isn't just about survival—it should be about legacy and prosperity.

And if Jewish communities can balance faith with financial success, Black communities can too.

Chapter 8: Moving Forward – Real Strategies for Change

If We Know What Works, Why Aren't We Doing It?

At this point, we've broken down the blueprint that Jewish communities use to build and sustain wealth:

- They teach financial literacy from childhood.
- They prioritize business ownership over just getting a "good job."
- They keep their money circulating within their community.
- They strategically invest in education and careers that generate wealth.
- They structure marriage and family planning around economic stability.
- They combine faith with action, not just blind hope.

Meanwhile, Black communities are still playing economic defense, stuck in cycles of:

- Paycheck-to-paycheck survival.
- Endless student loan and consumer debt.

CHAPTER 8: MOVING FORWARD – REAL STRATEGIES FOR CHANGE

- Little to no generational wealth transfer.
- Spending habits that make other communities rich first.

The good news is that change doesn't require luck, handouts, or a miracle. It just requires strategy, discipline, and execution.

Let's lay out a step-by-step action plan that Black communities can implement starting today.

1. Financial Literacy Must Start at Home

Jewish kids learn money principles before they even touch a dollar.

- By age ten, they understand saving, investing, and how money grows.
- By age eighteen, they know how to manage credit, start a business, and invest.

Compare that to Black communities, where:

- Most financial lessons come from trial and error.
- Talking about money is often seen as "grown folks' business."
- Many don't learn about investing or credit until after they've already made financial mistakes.

Action Steps:

- Start teaching kids about money early—allowance, budgeting, and saving.
- Introduce basic investing principles before age eighteen.

- Teach credit, business ownership, and wealth-building strategies at home.

2. Shift from a Job Mindset to an Ownership Mindset

Jewish families prioritize business ownership. Black families prioritize job security.

This is why:

- Jewish households have a higher percentage of entrepreneurs.
- Black workers are overrepresented in low-wage industries that don't build wealth.

(Source: U.S. Census Bureau, Small Business Administration)

A good job alone will never create wealth—but owning assets will.

Action Steps:

- Encourage entrepreneurship early—even if it's a side hustle.
- Teach kids that ownership (businesses, real estate, stocks) is the real goal.
- Stop relying solely on "job security"—it's never truly secure.

3. Keep Money in the Black Community Longer

The Jewish dollar circulates up to thirty times before leaving the community.

The Black dollar leaves in six hours.

(Source: Nielsen Consumer Report, 2023)

We don't need to boycott other businesses—we need to prioritize our own first.

Action Steps:

- Shop Black-owned first whenever possible.
- Bank with Black-owned institutions that reinvest in the community.
- Start group investments (family lending circles, business funding pools).

4. Invest in Strategic Education, Not Just College for the Sake of It

Jewish families don't just send their kids to college—they guide them into high-earning fields.

Meanwhile, Black students are encouraged to "just go to college" with no strategy.

This is why:

- Jewish graduates accumulate less student debt and earn higher salaries.
- Black graduates are more likely to take on excessive debt for degrees with low returns.

Action Steps:

- Only take on college debt if it leads to a high-income career.
- Consider trade schools, certifications, and entrepreneurship over useless degrees.
- Plan for education with a return on investment—don't just

go to school to "figure it out."

5. Prioritize Homeownership Over Lifetime Renting

- Seventy percent of Jewish households own homes.
- Less than forty-five percent of Black households own homes.

(Source: U.S. Census Bureau, 2023)

Jewish families help their kids buy homes early—Black families often expect their kids to figure it out alone.

Renting for life means paying someone else's mortgage forever.

Action Steps:

- Prioritize homeownership as early as possible (even a small property is better than none).
- Pool resources with family or friends to buy property.
- Stop financing liabilities (cars, luxury brands) and start building assets.

6. Stop Playing the Lottery with Faith—Use It to Build, Not Just Hope

Faith should be an economic tool, not a crutch.

Jewish communities use religious teachings to reinforce financial planning, investing, and community reinvestment.

Black churches often teach faith as a waiting game instead of an action plan.

Action Steps:

- Use faith to build wealth, not just endure poverty.
- Demand financial literacy programs in churches.
- Tithe strategically—give where it will create real impact.

7. Plan for Generational Wealth Transfer

Jewish families ensure their kids inherit businesses, real estate, and investment portfolios.

Black families often pass down nothing but debt and funeral costs.

Action Steps:

- Create a will and estate plan to ensure assets stay in the family.
- Buy life insurance—even a small policy can provide financial security.
- Start family trusts or investment accounts for future generations.

Final Thought: The Future Is in Our Hands

The Jewish wealth-building strategy is not magic—it's method.

- They learn financial literacy early.
- They prioritize ownership over just having a job.
- They keep their money circulating within their community.
- They strategically invest in education, marriage, and family stability.

- They plan generational wealth transfer.

Black communities can do the same.

This book wasn't written to complain about the past—it was written to create a blueprint for the future.

No more excuses. No more waiting.

The system was built against us—but we don't have to play by its rules.

It's time to build our own.

Conclusion: They Did It. So Can We.

This book wasn't written to preach. It was written to wake people up.

You've seen the playbook. The blueprint. The facts. Jewish communities didn't wait for perfect conditions. They didn't wait for handouts. They didn't ask permission to build wealth. They just did it—quietly, consistently, and strategically.

And no, it wasn't luck. It was deliberate financial literacy. Family structure. Ownership. Investment. Community-first thinking. A formula that anyone can follow if they stop looking for shortcuts and start playing the long game.

Meanwhile, Black communities are out here with more talent, more hustle, and more influence—but we're still outspent, out-owned, and out-planned. Why? Because no one handed us the blueprint. Until now.

Let's be clear: the system was never designed for us to win. But here's the truth nobody likes to say out loud—

You don't have to play by the system's rules if you build your own.

So here's the final call:

- Stop waiting for things to be fair.
- Start circulating money where it matters.

- Build something your kids can inherit.
- Raise the bar from survival to ownership.

No more saying "We don't have anything."

No more celebrating one rich celebrity like that's the finish line.

No more excuses.

You already have the knowledge.

Now it's about execution.

They did it.

So can we.

And if we don't? That's on us.

Made in the USA
Coppell, TX
20 May 2025